THE DAY EVERY DAY IS

LEE UPTON

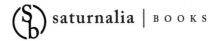

saturnalia | BOOKS

Distributed by Independent Publishers Group
Chicago

Saturnalia Books
105 Woodside Rd.
Ardmore, PA 19003
info@saturnaliabooks.com

ISBN: 978-1-947817-50-0 (print), 978-1-947817-51-7 (ebook)
Library of Congress Control Number: 2022947310

Cover artwork and book design by Robin Vuchnich

Distributed by:
Independent Publishing Group
814 N. Franklin St.
Chicago, IL 60610
800-888-4741

for Eric, always

CONTENTS

1.

THE IDEA

We couldn't get away from the idea,
and the idea wouldn't learn anything new.
Loyal like certain saints.
Always a saint but never a martyr.
The idea covered the sky in a web, invisible,
never yet seen by anyone—
until one night we actually saw the idea.
We saw the idea when it was attacked in a crowd.
The idea turned frightened eyes our way.
We destroyed ourselves to protect it.

POLITICAL AMBITION

A pig swallowing an entire
apple tree
then sleeping under covers
Politics must be hard
You can't step into
the same politics twice
I take off my boots
When I try to put them back on
they won't let me
Politics is wearing them now
Politics can always step into a victim twice
Here's Pharaoh
here's a basket
and inside the basket
is the death of Pharaoh's son.

THE APOLOGY

Tonight outside the plate glass
each insect is made of a long tube of wood,
as if the insect had become a tree
to give the tree a voice.
And these pink spatters,
these crumbled parlor doilies,
these milkweed blossoms
fade as if antique,
and the milkweed does not report on the condition of its leaves,
the height of its flowers,
its life without bureaucracy,
nor does the lilac filtering the mentholated air,
or the bee drowsing on the sill
after straining through the broken window screen
like Rilke wheedling his way into a palace.
Or the brook that runs by the cabin
talking nonsense.
Or the willow that slouches as if it were in a classroom
where the teacher bores it.
So forgive me please already.
I am sorry for speaking for nature.
But it was asking for it.

MARSYAS'S MUSIC

*—After losing a musical contest with Apollo, the satyr Marsyas
was skinned alive. In some versions of the story, Marsyas was
the true winner.*

The dog violet, pressing a flat ear to the ground,
has news of great importance:
it is spring
and jealousy turns its blade again.
First a nick at the neck and another nick and then
Marsyas's eyelids are peeled
so he can't help but see as
they flay the fur off him
and pull down the map of his body
and curry his skin.
Steam hisses off the oiled husks of him.
What do the executioners expect to find,
unwrapping their prize?
They take their time slitting his groin,
calling him a woman and laughing.
His blood rains into the storm-blue eye of the violet.
They work at his thighs
until the flesh
slides to his ankles like a stocking.

His hooves dance in the sloughed off rind.
There are jokes.
Even as the onrush from what's loosened gives,
as if a musician must be
poured from a kettle, but first
scalped, grated,
scraped into paste,
oh he's bled—he's dressed like a doe in a shed—
until saddles of his own skin surround him.

Thus, the satyr became human,
as did his torturers,
as did music.

Every spring the dog violet shrinks closer to the earth,
once again washed
in the thundercloud of
Marsyas's body,
and so the violet turns humble,
spreading its kind across the grounds to escape
the punishment for making beauty
humiliate a power

that won't be humbled.
Skinless, to be human,
to break membranes,
fear wiping its hands over your eyes,
and now so many silences:
those we can't hear
and those we try not to hear
and those beneath
what's heard.
In some myths,
a reed or laurel or blossom
fills to the brim with a soul.
In this story silence pours into silence,
and silence turns into music made of silence—

What will hold the dog violets back this year?
A scout has broken from the ranks.
The leaves flicker with Marsyas.
He was an animal, like us.

The extinct, those that no longer
bend down the grasses

or the tree tops or
curl in a wave
or draw their roots into the soil—
Marsyas and his kind are extinct.
Apollo is extinct.

Beside the limestone quarries the cry violets
lifted their lavender-colored faces:
the cry violets are extinct.
The earthly music of the extinct,
those wild beings skimmed off the earth,
scoured—
the blade so thin
and the scald—
in the encyclopedia of the extinct,
and in human music, that silence.
The satyr's skin drying, tacked to a pine:
the tattery flag of the extinct.
He was not our savior, not a traitor either.
We can only try to imagine Marsyas's music,
his gift.
We are his skin now,

his animals, his herd.
That music,
the wound in the dog violet,
the stillness there,
as if whatever thing that lives in silence
witnesses how living skin
is thrashed
wild with misery.
It is always happening:
the persistence of torture,
the extinguished music,
the ones made strange to us
skimmed off the earth.

The grass turns gray,
the decayed trees creak like wicker.
Executioners
stand back
to admire their work.
Wasps crawl
across a tender body, a body
made infinitely more tender

in sunlight,
the heart still beating.
Some traditions hate us.

What do we call
those who went ahead,
our scouts, the extinct?
They didn't ask to be named.
Now we know them only as words.
Marsyas, revolutionary, belongs to us and the other animals.
The animals of ourselves listen
for his flaying,
the blade pressing up against
every shape his mouth makes.
A thousand traps cannot snare the spring
or close his raining eyes
or stop the wind through
the pines howling.

REGRETS

I'm sorry for the gnus, their silent letter.

Sorry for the guns, no silencers.

Sorry you keep bullets in your sock drawer.

Sorry about the island under the sea.

Sorry about the small faced flowers

crushed by stones.

Sorry I never wrote an elegy for elegies.

Sorry I watched a man put his head in a lion's mouth

and the mouth was a country.

WAR ELEPHANTS

The armored, lance-tusked elephants of Rome, the elephants of Carthage
        crush enemy after enemy.
        On the back of each trumpeting elephant
        the javelin throwers, the exquisite archers—
the elephants plowing through the awed enemy,
        the soft-eyed
        poor-sighted elephants,
        thousands of muscles in each trunk—
until the enemy's lightest riders
        on the quickest horses and carrying torches
        dash among the elephants,
        blinding and terrifying them—
and the elephants turn,
        crushing their own army,
        the way terror turns—
        and drives through us, raging.

HYACINTH

*—Hyacinth: killed, by accident or out of anger, by a discus
thrown by his lover*

And always after one murder or another
a great power wonders,
how shall I commemorate the act?
Already the boy is frightened as the stone speeds

from a god's fingertips and
sweeps through the air to his temple
—stunned. Irreversible
the moment the sky opened to kill him.

The power that hurled his death was stung,
but continued on, although saddened,
and sent to the funeral these
blood drops, plump, sleeved in green.

Early spring, snow still on the ground,
and what's alive shivers. Chilled:
a body was here: a chisel,
rooting upward into fragrance,

a petition of grief, washed in icy silt.
The scent drifts,
a little rebellion but not justice,
wrung from a wound.

WHAT ELSE

"What else to do / but drive a small dog / out of yourself / with a stick?"
—Miroslav Holub, trans. David Young
and Dana Hábová

When the dog goes out
the cat comes in.
How to find a spot of sun?
A nap by the open window.
The delicate washing up.
And what to do next
but drive out
the stick?

AFTER BLOGGING ABOUT SHIRLEY JACKSON'S "THE LOTTERY"

Before I posted about

Tessie Hutchinson's apron I read

Ruth Franklin's biography

The room in which I began to read the biography was red

and on the wall: a reproduction of a

tapestry

The tapestry's sky pricked into blooms

where the ground is the sky

Later the moths and rot attempted their entry

You can't put a tapestry in "The Lottery"

The imagination refuses

Tessie Hutchinson cannot have a unicorn

A tapestry looks nothing like

the world she knew

the humans the animals

the sky blossoms

In Jackson's work

a brisk voice rises

to the brim of the language

It is June again

It would take more than a unicorn to turn

the stones back

In the tapestry a woman holds a mirror

to the unicorn

And the unicorn can only

see a part of himself

He looks like an alpaca somewhat

The unicorn is pure and may rest in a girl's lap

If he's restless

she will be harmed

Everyone must already

be harmed in Jackson's plot

How many lotteries

has Tessie Hutchinson watched

Since childhood

how many stones has she thrown

If she hadn't picked the slip of paper

with the black spot

would she have murdered

with the others

her own child

She wipes her hands on her apron

Her dishes weren't left in the sink

To be taught to ignore

the imagination—years of that teaching
Tenderness and awe—how I feel about some authors
As if Shirley Jackson were a unicorn
June is the month of the moth settling in
In Jackson's story without a rescue or a miracle
a community
does not exclude even the smallest child
from murder and murdering
and we hurry to read through the story because
we would not be forgiven
for being late
and slide in among the crowd
How familiar it all is—
choosing what to ignore
and everyone expecting
us to be responsible
and to do our part
The entire crowd waiting
while we hurry
almost forgetting what day every day is.

DANAË

*—Raped by Zeus who appeared as a shower of gold, Danaë and
her infant son were confined in a wooden chest and dropped into
the sea, as commanded by her father who feared the prophecy that
his grandchild would kill him*

My child was made of luck and money,
although I was unlucky,

for we were stuffed into a drawer
meant to sink. My brow

grew raw from knocking.
We were tossed for so long

I feared our coffin would break,
my child tucked against my lungs

and my mind nearly gone.
When at last we floated ashore

the lid was crow-barred
and there we were, salt lipped,

like something dried and nailed to a board.
They had to stretch my legs, unclasp

my fingers from my infant's back.
We sucked the leafy air into our mouths,

and I pretended to forget, to be harmless,
in my arms innocence.

Did I tell anyone what my child
was capable of? Did I brag?

I knew worlds would turn to stone,
many torn from home, for centuries.

Let murderers drive you into the sea
and wash their hands. For a while your silence

will fool them. Your child's.
You tell yourself as much.

Call it an accident or revenge or
an act of war that killed

my child's grandfather—
or memory's milk gone sour.

THE GHOST PIPE

Sunshine spans through the Queen Anne's lace,
        a field of headless ruffs.
Whereas no need for light
        for the ghost pipe,
Persephone's daughter,
        crimped in place
on her throne of roots, her fingerbones clammy.
        She sprang from dank soil,
her frayed wedding dress
        doused in rotting ice—
the pallor of disease and emptiness.
        At the end of her stems
faces are nodding around a death bed.
        And yet spotting her
in the glitterless damp
        we turn back and kneel.
She is her mother's child, and so
        she learned to resist all
that defiled her mother.
        Pick a stem
and the ghost pipe collapses, rare and
        unpossessable and unpossessed.

A FRIENDSHIP

The prey animal in our house
sees in all directions,
except in front of his nose—
the blind spot.
I understand, my friend said,
why you're standing away from me.
She thought I could see her better that way.
In one of my dreams she lost a rabbit
and I spent the dream trying to find her
another rabbit.
Once, she told me she was so happy
she envied herself.
When the stranger's rifle went off
she could feel the air unzip beside her head.
Another time she came home to discover
two bullet holes above her headboard—
her brother had visited.
Years later a woman who resembled her
was struggling to cross the rain-flooded street.
When I tried to help
the woman screamed *Fuck off* and I did.
Even then I remembered what I felt

for my friend,

how early on I knew there was an end

to our friendship,

the door closing,

the bones adhering,

and I hated that there was

a season for everything.

TWO GIFTS OF MUSHROOMS IN TWO SACKS

I didn't trust the ones
        smuggled for us
purportedly
        from the forests of Europe,
weathered, desiccated flesh,
        and in what soil exactly
had these grown
        and who plucked them
—we didn't know,
        or those others delivered by another friend,
some species never tasted
        we kept imagining,
or the fate of the taster
        unknown,
and some with a rind like a cantaloupe
        or enameled, and
others apparently polished
        like a rock in a tumbler
but soft necked.
        I registered many shades
and simulations
        at the bottom of the sack,

imagined their preferences

      for decay, their embarrassment

without orifices,

      the littler ones like chicken feed,

and then that smoke colored

      devil's horn snapped off,

and that flabby ear of a

      shrunken horse,

and that doorknob

      into the storm cellar

where we used to hunch

      during tornado warnings.

Each sack so darkly deep inside

      it seemed that if

the mushrooms tumbled out

      and I accidentally trampled them

I'd be cursed forever

      and wear a mask of measles

and run riot in a ditch

      and filibuster a hillside

and turn into one of their cousins,

      a known killer—.

Each bleached passport unstamped.

    What did we miss

that unplanned summer

    when a week apart these gifts arrived,

the interior of each sack

    like the stillness

inside a small painting,

    a forest folded inward,

enough for us to ask

    what other gifts are wasted on us?

FORCING FORSYTHIA

Setting the vase in window light
to make forsythia believe it's spring.
All because we want the yellowing touch of sunlight in the house,
a minor crime,
like not being truthful when you say you're fine
to a friend fooled by warmth.
Saying less to mean anything at all.

THE ROLLED AWAY STONE

The women came upon the tomb
and the stone was rolled away.
They could not know how
except that it had been done,
if their grief moved the stone.
They knew he hadn't been alive.
They knew even more than the soldiers
after the lance entered his side.
They had washed his hands and feet,
wrung out a cloth over his eyelids,
and now the body was gone.
They didn't imagine the body stolen.
No, the body walked out.
God so loved the body.

OUR ICE

The nets silvery docked, and the portholes frosted,
        the white pond scum and duck weed,

and the pine's greenness
        frosted like a forged dollar bill

or the newsprint color of corpses in ancient paintings,
        the chilled twine crackling upward

like forgetfulness,
        which is our second language, a honeycomb

frozen in veiny reaches
        crawling over the past,

that seabird webbed in ice,
        and we dream of the thaw,

at last the hyacinth curled
        as if stemmed by a current,

and the bee, that free citizen
        of the short lived empire,

his star-flecked coat unstiffening,

     or our faces pressed against the lake's ice

listening for the thaw,

     the hard roar of all we can't express.

2.

ACTORS

We give our hours away to them
        as if our hours aren't magnificent.
They murder and autopsy one another.
        They echo our secret ideologies,
and if you listen closely
        you hear the under-soliloquy.
We're all actors, nearly everyone says.
        We want to say:
Pure pain doesn't pretend.
        They say, for a long run,
the same words
        over and over again. So do I. How are you?
I'm fine. I'm fine. I'm fine.
        I'm playing pain.
I'm playing pain again.

WHAT DID HELEN DO?

She crossed the avenue
of creation and set the channel
changer under the couch

She kicked out the lights
on the van, wish-boned the hill peaks and
hallucinated feathers

While the vengeful battered
the walls of her adopted town
she bathed in sludge

not once forgetting
how she first pecked out of a shell
peeping and peeping

and couldn't see herself as she was—
she never possessed
a decent mirror

For ten years
to endure all that clamor—
to be like a horse-drawn wagon

or a gun pulled again and again out of a drawer—
for what? for what? for what?
and finally

to be returned, loose change,
to her husband
like the years could be unspun

Oh it can't be depicted
as it must have
been done

the way torture
is never depicted
by touch.

PRIVACY

I like a private life, it's true.
Sometimes it's so private if I say something that's even a little bit arguably private
I feel disdain for myself.

I remember how cruel people were to my mother when she was going blind,
how even one of her doctors lied disdainfully,
keeping part of her diagnosis private.
Privacy is a kind of power, that must be obvious.

Who cares? one of my friends said.
I tell everyone everything about myself, she said.
And that's when I knew she was the one
who told my secret.

I am baring to you my privacy
not by admitting all the shameful things I've done
especially those when I thought
I was being moral, uncompromising, right.

The one man I heard speak about the power of transparency
caused so much suffering I shudder
when I hear his name.
Right now, by talking about privacy

I'm giving up the secret
of my great weakness, how much
privacy means to me
although apparently it must not mean much

given that I'm not being private about it.
A woman moved closer to us because
she found my nephew attractive.
I've substituted other nouns and pronouns for the correct ones

in the above statement.
Today I'm wearing a big CONFIDENTIAL
sign around my neck.
I've lived long enough to know enough

to keep my mouth shut—I wrote down those words
years ago
so that I would forget them.
In the gallery the man said,

"I look at that painting of a barn
and I can just about smell the hay."
And those strawberries and the lemons,
the rind on that lemon stripped,

the curl of it.
I see that and I can
just about smell the gin.
I'm thinking about light at dusk, last light

that brings on thoughts I battle with.
If I were more romantic
I'd say demons
except they're bodiless.

The spread of sunshine
inside that onion
or the turrets inside the lemon
do not dim although hidden.

I put on a rind myself.
A still life is not still.
It is baring itself.

IF MUSIC

"If music be the food of love, play on,
Give me excess of it; that surfeiting,
The appetite may sicken, and so die."

—*Twelfth Night*

I had read the lines too young to know
much of what they meant
and as such I was
sacrificed on pure sound
I mis-remembered: If music be the *meat* of love—
which seems no less impossible
Music of that kind I've known
and it did not feed love enough
for love to sicken and die
I understand
when a cure is needed
I have my love
The fear one of us will sicken and die—
that fear feeds from love.

THE GOD OF MEDICINE

Amazon asks me to rate
my recent purchase of "vomit bags."
I'm not tempted to do so.
No, I only want the god of medicine
to come down to visit.
He doesn't ask forgiveness.
Maybe he should.
He wants our patience.
He's learning, he says, and
you are gambling, he says.
You're fortunate to be able to gamble.
Think of your ancestors
riding so early to death.
Look at him now,
leaning on his elbows.
He must know he needs luck and prayers—
he's too often the only helpless god.

ACTAEON'S TESTIMONY

I couldn't see any of the skin on her,
not so much as a dimple,
for the water kept flashing in sequins and spangles,
and right then everything retracted,
and I knew, just the same,
my heart halfway out my back
in fear, that she wouldn't have seen me,
shocked and turning away,
if her followers hadn't spotted me first,
flashed their hands and raised a cry.
I stepped in it, that was for sure.
You don't insult some people
with your common human presence.
First, though,
the weight came down on my head,
their accusations branching
as antlers, and even when I howled apologies
the ones I fed who used to follow me
saw blood to charge,
and they were on my heels, nipping,
then snapping toward my neck.
They'd have my head, my lungs ransacked,

they were wagging over
what was left of me.
What I endured—
it's always happening,
the shrieking and then the chase.
Innocence did not save me.
Remember that
when you're accused and cursed
because of the crime of wandering into
that place where power felt secure, all tucked away,
taking a little bath with her friends.
Remember when power sends its hounds.
You wouldn't recognize yourself either,
not in their telling of it.

EURYDICE: MY TURN

The same story again and again:
I'm between two men,
and it's all about them.
Why is it my husband's choice?
Why is it his view, and his voice?
Of course, after those women tore him apart,
his head went on singing—
and you never heard from me again.
Frankly, he should have torn himself apart.

CATALOGUE

I hardly had a name for what happened.
Silence doesn't cover it.
Only years later I began to understand
and like Homer with his catalogue of ships
I made a list:
choking
kicking
spit.
Strangers and not-strangers,
named and no name known.
And now I think about how safe I am although
there's always that sensation
like the way some of us endure
ringing in the ears:
how there could have been someone
who murdered you like the girl from the cafeteria,
someone who noticed someone else first.
And then going back to when I was a child,
the teacher who struck the back of my hand with a stick,
and how I wanted to grow tall like a tree or become a fence.
No wonder I loved the myths.
They spoke every language we lived.

THE CHECK

Before I sign a check
I have to pause
       to remember my name.
I don't identify with my name
though I've never changed it.
       I was born into it,
but why should it be different from my face
which I was born into
       and which keeps changing?
We might be better for changing names,
meeting this stranger
       who ought to be given a chance again
and then another chance.
Maybe we'd be less quick to judge
       every citizen of the empire.
Maybe we'd quietly watch
the sea breaking over
       a stone gate,
every night breaking
on a new name
       and we'd occasionally remember
our first names

in our first lives,

    and refuse to condescend to them,
unlike the way we treat old age.

THE SPIREA

Sometimes I think of what it was like:
      hiding behind the spirea,
the clotted cream of blossoms
      where I stayed quiet, still.
I would be ignored there
      in the spirea, and later I'd hide
farther from the house
      with the jello of roses, the putty of anemones
in the watery air among the leaves.
      Then I'd hurry back to the spirea
where I was hidden most.
      I knew I couldn't continue always
in the rusting lace,
      the miniscule lesions at the end of each branch.
Although I was lonely
      I didn't want God to hide with me.
Yet sometimes he came and settled himself
      in the veil of spirea,
and I believed he almost understood and I
      wouldn't be judged.
I would be kindly forgotten. Until,
      like the spirea,
he shed himself, dry snow
      tossed on grass.

THE SUNFLOWER

When I was in my twenties
I used to wash the same blouse in the sink
three nights in a row
so I could keep wearing it.
I liked that blouse that much

although it didn't bring me luck.
I'd lie on the couch that was my bed
with books around me, my hands stuttering to sleep.
I'd wake up, ink on ink.
I was like someone who burns down a barn—

full of contrition
for the crime and for being in love with the hay.
I didn't know how not to trust strangers.
I met a man who chastised me for being happy.
Being serious: what he wanted from me.

I became like one of those sunflowers whose heavy head
perpetually bends to the dirt.
I denied I was happy. The truth was:
even when some of the worst happened
one part of me was happy. I hid my happiness

as if I knew I would need it later

and like anyone I did. I never liked sunflowers

until my mother asked for them. When she was losing her sight

they were what she could see.

THE DINNER

He left me in the restaurant. First,
        he stood over the table shouting.
The owner came out, sad eyed,
        and put the dish I'd ordered
in front of me. Her pity
        was embarrassing.
Soon the other diners
        returned to their conversations.
My eyes ached and I couldn't eat.
        Gradually, something inside me
began to shift, little pins pulling away
        from my skin, or maybe
the feeling was like
        legs coming unstuck
from a hot car seat.
        Before I could eat
he returned, bringing cold air on his coat,
        and sat down
opposite me again.
        That's when I knew I had to be careful
and make a plan
        and that I should be afraid.

His violence was well ordered and
        discrete. I slid
my plate toward him,
        my adversary.

BLUE FLOWERS

To be extinct in slow motion
a blue lung skinned
as if a being
must be bailed out and here's
the tender hide
I thought we would pour the water later
let the heliotrope make
its place with
the pool on the spent lip
of the hyacinth
the bundles of snowfall flowers
each gasp shedding
toward the raindrop
on the window
where ice will envy
glass for long life
and glass envies ice—
that it moves
The blue flowers envy
no others
to be born without thorns
hanging from the

stem of the world
Like the Vikings,
the bees die with their swords.

THE NAMING

I looked up into the tree,
to the rounded globes,
some were green,
only one was russet.
I named colors, textures.
Please give me the adjectives at least.
That's what I asked.
What I saw was sparkling streaked
and heavy weighing the branch.
I didn't need a voice to tell me
to pluck what I wasn't
supposed to need.
Before then we all fed on air.
Even the leaves were not
tucking themselves away from us—
until I tore at
the world's skin as brittle
as a snake's.
Afterwards
I needed a snake's spine
to walk upright.
Then my kind offer

to the only other living human:
a bite.
Next: banishment, exile.
I had no choice:
I wanted a child.

AN EPIC FOR MOTHER'S DAY

Epic: "a poem including history"

—Ezra Pound

A poem with history
a history with poems in it
in history with a poem
a history with short lives in it
a history of the needle and wrench and cable
and a pretty dress and a grave
and a pretty dress in a grave
roll the stone from the grave
raise the corpse and breathe into her mouth
take Ovid from the shelf and change shapes in history
in history with a poem on a cushion or in a field
or on a swing or force fed
in a house or a trench
a body that pushes history out.

THE DOUBTER

While wrapping gifts, folding
a sheet of paper, knotting a ribbon,
I think of those I've loved who died,
and I think too of doubting Thomas
who put his hand inside
the wound of a man he believed
could not be alive.

To walk beside a man and slip your hand in his side,
the intimacy of it,
a divine body, a mortal body,
did Thomas's hand return to him
flayed?

A wound went on a rampage
through a body.
The lit-up places
where the wound traveled—
I once owned a vase like a wound that wouldn't heal.
The pattern included open lattice work.
Only good for emptiness or dried flowers.

A wound asks to be cleaned first.
Maybe—I can't doubt—some misery
has to do with the need
to defend ourselves from the doubting
hands of others—
to keep our doubts, to keep a hand inside
our own wound,
not believing in the wounds of others.

THE BLANKET

How often
I place a blanket
over my sleeping daughters
and know my arms are
my mother's and her mother's and her mother's.
How often my mother
turned on a light
beside me as I read,
fearing I'd ruin my eyes
although she herself went blind.
How often she asked if I needed
an extra blanket
and skimmed her hand over
the top of my head.
I do the same with my own daughters
just as my mother's mother and her mother did.
As if the afterworld is the body.

CALLING FOR HER

Not a day goes by
that I don't call for her.
Do I think my mother is endangered.
She's beyond danger, isn't she?
In December my daughters and I walk by the ocean.
The wind scours our faces.
The waves encroach and then draw back
like forgetfulness, whose first language is memory.

HOW STRANGE

The first stone—
how strange that no one cast the first?
How strange that those people put down their stones.
How strange: the silence that overtook the crowd.

THE FALLEN ANGELS

They skimmed off the skin
of paradise, falling
like honey twirling
on a wooden spool
until their wings must
have been slashed
into the crispest clouds,
their claws stiffened
into door hinges,
and they were never forgiven, falling
perpetually, muscling the air.
How could we not have made them
in our image?
For we've fallen
on a driveway, we've fallen
in a parking lot. We've fallen
where there was nothing to make us fall.
I myself have fallen
in snow, on ice, on ice-lessness. I've fallen
before I learned to walk.
I've fallen
in crowds and alone. I've caught myself

on a chair and fell
with the chair.
I un-grasped the air.
I flattened. Un-spared,
I neglected to stay standing.
I can't pretend I ever was knocked out of
the littlest bit
of heaven. So much flailing,
hoping to be blameless.
Look at us, falling
with every fault, every
failing we can't keep hidden.
Even Mary mother of God
lost her own child
at the temple—
for days.
Who are we
not to be forgiven?

3.

THE REPRIEVE

March grew
until the underworld was endless.
Sometimes after work I walked
to the dollar store.
I gave myself a budget: $2.
One day I bought saltshakers
shaped like a Dutch boy and girl.
On the way back to my apartment
where I lived above a man with a dying dog
I walked past a magnolia—
buds like litter in the tree.
And then a thought I'd never thought
occurred to me:
As long as I live I will never wear wooden shoes.
And that was the moment when
I felt again the stirrings
of friendliness toward my life.

PRODIGAL

Why love the prodigal
Why should anyone
Or is it love?
The story is not about love
or forgiveness

I didn't want to leave
or I wanted to leave
I had to get out
They forced me out
Stay and I'd be dead
Never ask why I left
Not even what I did afterwards

I understand resentment
the no good
the last to enlist
the first to run away
But how could I understand
the big welcome back party?

I had slipped out
right when the knife
twisted against the hinge
Nevertheless, I was always going
to come back
I couldn't leave
without returning
without seeing for once

the mountain's reflection in the pearl—
Leaving and returning
is what a prodigal does.
It is her poetry.

GRIEF INSTRUCTION

The Italian noblewoman
who during all her travels required
that the corpse of the saint
be carried with her in a glass case—
I want to tell my children:
Don't let me be your luggage after my death.
No sense dragging me through churches.
I did enough of that in my lifetime.

AN OFFENSE

The famous poet said
to the woman his own age,
Let's hear your pretty flower poems.
I looked at her grave face.
I still see her all these years later, how she stood up.
I wanted anger to leap inside her poems,
for her roses to swarm over a wall and break down the brick.
She didn't read anything at all like that.
Her poem was long.
Very long. Remarkably long.
She buried him, buried him in roses.

KNOWLEDGE

When the thing crawled from behind the drain plate
       I clamored out of the tub
and threw on a towel. Slowly, sensing my presence,
       the centipede shrank back.
Just like that, from above, God
       must have seen Adam and Eve
as faceless, shuddering,
       anxious to hide.
I have thought for years about
       the done and the undone
and how the undone may be
       our paradise.
Every leg of the centipede
       preserves a rare form
of intelligence. How strange we must seem
       to God. How sometimes we must
frighten him, how he must wish we would just
       crawl away. And then he has to
forgive himself for being squeamish.
       He was the one who first saw us naked.

OILS

In the corner a wren is pecking about
like a poet working in a forgotten language.
Wind turns the curtains wild
and sunlight taps the canvas,
blanching the wren. Wait
and the wren comes back
like those beings assumed to be extinct
that turn up, only one of their kind,
before vanishing again.
Next to disappear:
the pear with a dimple
polished by syrup
and the dried riverbed on a crust of bread.
These old paintings,
no one has any idea who made them.
They wrinkle like figs.

SNAPDRAGONS AT THE MARKET

I wish I'd taken you
out of the bucket
and brought you home.
Which way would the sun
flow into the room
for your clocks?
You drank a bee
and it stung your lips.
Or are those jawbones
or paws
on your stems,
or curdled grudges?
As if anyone could own you.
For the second night
I am still thinking of you
even as sleep comes with its
soft little sack.
You own me, I suppose.

DOING THE BILLS

My father impaling bills
on a nail on a block of wood
then putting his head in his hands
and you with your head in your hands
and my head in my hands
hands over my eyes
and I see again what I forgot for decades
my father
after doing the bills
crumbling bread in a bowl
and pouring milk over the bread
and spooning in sugar.

ALE & CAKES

"Dost thou think because thou art virtuous
there shall be no more cakes and ale?"

—Twelfth Night

It's not all cakes and ale.
>Sometimes it's ale and cakes.
At least one of us knew his ale and cakes.
>He could poach your deer
to accompany your ale and cakes.
>He could hold up his side
in a knife-in-your-eye tavern fight.
>Ale will give you courage.
Cake will give you cake.
>So have some cake. With ale.
Sing happy birthday
>to your birthday cake.
Your virtue's not meant to span
>from cradle to grave,
not when you're made of cake,
>and not when you're made of ale.
It's not all cakes and ale.
>It's not all aches and suffering.
So much is made of cake.

The ale takes care of itself.
It's not all cakes and ale.
      Sometimes it's ale and cakes.
Virtue is often faked.
      We all ought to know.
There's more in a bar or a bakery
      than are dreamt of
in your theocracy.

THE MORAL ARBITER

appears in every age
appears in us
looking out
with a squint
of certainty toward the
impure heart
and there is always, always
something for the ladies,
for instance:
the dunking stool.
At last we got
to sit down.

THE MAJOR HOLIDAYS

—in memory of James Tate

The whole time I almost forgot about Unwise-mas, Unthink-mas,
and the Festival of Sullenness,
and how they all fell this year
in the month of the Day of Reckoning
and the Eve of Canceled Reservations. And then
Padma came over on Retribution Monday
and wanted to know if we were going to have our usual party on
Happy Hour All Eve Saturday. That's when we said
it was unlikely because of a conflict: the next day was
Unholy Mother-in-Law Arbor Cataclys-mas.
But then, what do you know, Tony said: Let's check the calendar—
don't forget The New Moon's Shakespeare Fest.
No, I said, correctly, that's the Festival of Too Many Boxed Fish.
You're looking at August. Plus,
the Equinox of Noxiousness is right around the corner
and the Laughing Sanitation Primary, and
pretty soon we'll hit right up against
The Hefty Food Poisoning Centennial,
and It's Obvious I Need To Parade My Pony with a President Anniversary,
and—oh no, I just about neglected to remember
Whistle Pig Appreciation Day.
The other days—they have names probably—
but those I mentioned,
those are the major holidays.

WHY AM I NOT INVITED TO YOUR PARTY?

And what are your parties like without me?
Dancing? Is there dancing?
I used to dance. I danced like someone being stung
by ferocious bees. Agony was my means. I danced
to words I've never said aloud:
like *scullery* and *larder.*
And whenever what was playing stopped
I poured myself back into my body
like a deer at the side of a highway turning
away from the impulse to cross.
And exactly because I was all over the grid
someone left the party
saddled in the biggest gleaming body, hooved.
So if you keep me off your party list
I guess I can't make myself understand.
More than once I sacrificed my dignity
on the slab of a kitchen island.
More than once I danced off the cliff
and let everyone, first, jump from my back.
It was what we call wonderful, wasn't it?
It was. That's what it was.

MUCHNESS

"You've lost your muchness"
—often falsely attributed to Lewis Carroll; the line
comes from Tim Burton's *Alice in Wonderland*

It's been so long since the muchness lost me
even though I felt around in the darkness where
the muchness used to hunt

back when muchness arrived at the door early
and I had so much muchness I turned away more.
By now, shouldn't there be another muchness

for all the words wasted
whenever I made too much of someone?
Where is my muchness that will turn

inside out whatever I was made of?
Muchness, why don't you knock on my door anymore?
Why don't you make yourself heard?

That's how we'll know you're our muchness.
Our lost muchness.
Not the new muchness. Not that again.

THE BEST DRINK

The afternotes: orange, a little frangipani,
and then something harsh and mineral:
an old jug rutted out of the ruins of a lost chapel.
But first it was like drinking spring water
lathed by rocks fatty with quartz.
No, it's inexplicable,
even the way that drink spared our feelings.
That drink liked loneliness and appreciation, lingering appreciation.
Just thinking about that drink creates a kind of yearning
that douses you like sea spray.
I drank that drink and was convinced my body
was flying of its own accord, and why not?
The myth of Icarus is an ugly story
retold and retold and retold
by someone resentful who wasn't able to drink
the best of the drinks we ever drank.
There was a clear sky in that glass and shaggy pines
and a bit of snowmelt doused in a fire,
and soon a blue shawl drew itself from the rim
and brimmed over us both, and something caught
inside our throats and was released—some old grief.
A grief that, possibly, didn't even come from us.
Or even from our ancestors.

HYSTERIA

My womb was floating and I was on it
like the Jetsons.
Hysterical laughter
driving on a highway.
Under the bridge hysteria.
What is the womb doing now, hysteria?
And the blackbirds baked in the pie—
they not only had to die
but entertain the king. Poor things!
Like glass dipped in a barrel of oil,
and the Vesuvius of each tiny headdress.
And now I keep intruding on a conversation
I'm having with myself.
It's irresponsible to despair.
And so I am hysterical enough for now.
Although I didn't always know hysteria was tapping a knife
all along the rim of my life.
I confess: I have so much practice in forgiving myself
even for hysterical gossip:
breaking into a greenhouse at night
and I can't see what I trample.
The stalks shattered,
the pots of soil overturned,

and yet the fragrance.

Hysteria inside the never opened book:

Dear book, you with your stiff love,

your breathless labors,

you who never gave birth to a reader.

FINISHING

I haven't wanted to think about making peace
      with yearning,
knowing that whatever I want finished,
      at some point, sooner now,
won't be finished.
      But maybe that will be all right,
after all?
      No. I'll wish for more time,
and then for more time.
      There will be something
I haven't finished,
      the ending I haven't ended.
And always, I will have tried,
      knowing I can't change the dream
in which a voice cried,
      You lost your chance.
I haven't been entirely scalded by that dream,
      and it was years ago, wasn't it?
Like holding back an avalanche
      with only two words: not yet.
When I was a four-year old
      the pink bracelet I cried for

was given instead to my sister.
I still remember it.
Even what I couldn't have
is what I have.

MY FJORD

I will sail through my own fjord and I will name the fjord My Fjord.
I know it's incorrect to say that the Vikings wore horned helmets,
but I will wear a horned helmet, for my job is to correct history.
I'll leap over vats of mead and let libations drench my puffy skirt.
(I like mead, but it's amazing how refreshing milk directly from the cow can be.)
And then I will sail on My Fjord plowing through every flaming
funeral. Enough celebrations of victory over life.
And who will stop my marauding?
For these are my violent decades,
and everyone everywhere from all time:
those are my own people.

UNDERWORLDERS

The forest stole silence
until cracking through the forest
came more of the forest,
the elderberries shining
or were those the shining eyes
of sparrows in the elderberries.

To walk through the woods
the woods walked out with us—
the thorns you made into a crown, dear one.

It's annoying when myths enter a poem by name
as if they're not there already.
To each her own underworld

and coming through shade—
a stranger in willows and fronds and mists,
not a human
but a body of earth and air:
the slow creek
        the mint on the bank
    the willowy overhang
                below which the minnows scatter…

I don't know if it's any less true
                    that this place is as much
what I am as my name or body.

Rain roars through a gully,
the rain that calls to us to stay inside,
how it must feel to the other animals
backing into the granary,
writhing inside a gunny sack.
The way the forest sways and breaks in waves.
The trees that become
the masts of ships the spines the laws and
decrees and licenses and indictments.
The boy in the house down the road
told a nurse
he thought the bullet was a bee sting.

Where is the hive
that is meant for all our bodies?

And who were these next shades?
And where is my family now?
Those people beyond legends?

No answer came,
except if fog is an answer,
except if my impatience drew that fog.

Somewhere the past is ahead of us
where those lost
are yet to be found.
This whole time on earth
was I looking for them
even when they were alive and with me?

Today I am holding my little girl's hand.
Across the road the elderberries wear sparrows
and next to the house that burned
we watch as
twin fawns take their steps,
beings that never yet knew loneliness.

ACKNOWLEDGMENTS

The author sincerely thanks the editors of the following journals in which some of these poems, sometimes under other titles and in other versions, first appeared:

The American Journal of Poetry: "The Doubter"

The Awl: "An Epic for Mother's Day"

Boston Review Online: "Marsyas's Music," republished in *Paws Healing the Earth*

Ecotone: "Two Gifts of Mushrooms in Two Sacks"

Field: Contemporary Poetry & Poetics: "Why Am I Not Invited to Your Party," republished in *New Poetry from the Midwest;* and "The Sunflower"

Florida Review: "The Idea" and "Regrets"

Georgia Review: "The Major Holidays"

Kenyon Review: "Our Ice"

Life & Legends: "Underworlders"

LitMag: "Political Ambition"

Los Angeles Review: "Hyacinth"

Massachusetts Review: "What Did Helen Do?"

The New Yorker: "The Apology," republished in *The Best American Poetry 2016;* "Privacy," featured on *The Slowdown;* and "Snapdragons at the Market"

Plume: "My Fjord"

Poem-a-Day from the Academy of American Poets: "The Best Drink"

Poetry: "Hysteria"

Poetry Northwest: "After Blogging about Shirley Jackson's 'The Lottery'"

Shenandoah: "Ale & Cakes"

Southern Review: "Doing the Bills," featured in *American Life in Poetry*"; and "An Offense"

Yale Review Online: "The Reprieve"

I'm grateful to the editorial team at Saturnalia Books, with special thanks to the marvelous poet Sarah Wetzel for her sensitive and invaluable editorial suggestions. My deep thanks to Sabrina Orah Mark for selecting the manuscript—and for her brilliant writing. Thanks as well to the artist Robin Vuchnich for creating the stunningly luminous cover of this book.

Many thanks to my colleagues and former students at Lafayette College: working with you has been a privilege.

Thanks to so many wonderfully supportive people, including Rosa Maria Arenas, Mik Awake, Steve Belletto, Alesia Betz, Paul Cefalu, Thom Crawford, Megan Fernandes, Alexis Fisher, Evan Fisher, Jennifer Gilmore, Marilyn Kann, Ed Kerns, Neil McElroy, Sheila McNamee, Jack McNamee, Maureen Mulrooney, Kirk O'Riordan, Carrie Rohman,

Emily Schneider, Randy Schneider, Beth Seetch, Diane Shaw, Rue-laine Stokes, Jim Toia, Walter Wadiak, Loring Wirbel, Yolanda Wisher, James Woolley, Susan Woolley, and Chuck Zovko.

Enduring gratitude to my fabulous sister Alice Faye, always loyal and steady and ready with her sense of humor—and with lasting thanks to my inspiring mother-in-law Yetta Ziolkowski.

I write in memory of my father Charles, my mother Rose, my brother Joe, my sister Lana, my niece Carla, and my father-in-law Theodore Ziolkowski.

I can't thank my daughters enough: Theodora, for her grace and generosity and splendid fiction and poetry; and CeCe, for comical, astute conversations, her valiant heart, and her powerful visual art.

And for Eric, to whom this collection is dedicated: amazing husband, father, and scholar—we've lived through miracles together.

AUTHOR BIOGRAPHY

Lee Upton's poetry has appeared widely, including in *The New Yorker, Poetry, The Southern Review*, and three editions of *Best American Poetry*. She is a fiction writer and literary critic as well as a poet. She has written six other collections of poetry, including *Bottle the Bottles the Bottles the Bottles*. She lives in Easton, Pennsylvania.

www.leeupton.com

Also by Lee Upton

Poetry
Bottle the Bottles the Bottles the Bottles
Undid in the Land of Undone
Civilian Histories
Approximate Darling
No Mercy
The Invention of Kindness

Fiction
Visitations: Stories
The Tao of Humiliation: Stories
The Guide to the Flying Island

Libretto
The Masque of Edgar Allan Poe

Essay Collection
Swallowing the Sea: On Writing & Ambition, Boredom, Purity & Secrecy

Critical Prose
Defensive Measures: The Poetry of Niedecker, Bishop, Glück, and Carson
The Muse of Abandonment: Origin, Identity, Mastery in Five American Poets
Obsession and Release: Rereading the Poetry of Louise Bogan
Jean Garrigue: A Poetics of Plenitude

The Day Every Day Is was printed in Adobe Caslon
www.saturnaliabooks.org